IMAGES
of America

PARKERSBURG

ON THE COVER: Parkersburg has hosted many famous faces throughout the years. Here, a group of actors enjoy the hospitality of William Henry "Wig" Bickel (left, nearest to feeder), whose menagerie was a major attraction in the area during his lifetime. (Courtesy of Artcraft Studio.)

IMAGES
of America

PARKERSBURG

Robert Anderson and Aaron Crites

ARCADIA
PUBLISHING

ISBN 978-1-5316-62868

Published by Arcadia Publishing
Charleston, South Carolina

Library of Congress Control Number: 2012935128

For all general information, please contact Arcadia Publishing:
Telephone 843-853-2070
Fax 843-853-0044
E-mail sales@arcadiapublishing.com
For customer service and orders:
Toll-Free 1-888-313-2665

Visit us on the Internet at www.arcadiapublishing.com

Rob — For my wife, Kelly, and our daughters, Shelby and Abby

Aaron — For my wife, Cheryl

CONTENTS

ACKNOWLEDGMENTS

Writing a short pictorial history was a daunting task: what to leave in . . . what to leave out? Several people made this an easier task. Paul Borrelli of Artcraft Studio deserves note first. His voluminous photograph archive and encyclopedic knowledge of Parkersburg's history are a treasure. Brian Kesterson also deserves a special note of thanks. Other contributors of photographs and knowledge who made our job easier were the Spencer family at Glendale Gym, Ken and Glenda Eaton, Kitty Brown, coaches Buddy James and Don Reeves, Chief Eric Taylor and Tina Sandy of the Parkersburg Fire Department (PFD), Dennis Bell at WVU at Parkersburg, Bill and Nordeen Yearego, Bob Enoch, and Suzy Gunter, among many others.

Several abbreviations will be used throughout this book, including PHS for Parkersburg High School, PSHS for Parkersburg South High School, and WVU at Parkersburg for West Virginia University at Parkersburg.

Never intending the book to be all encompassing and include only often-reviewed material, the authors chose to take the road less traveled. Some images will be familiar and some might spark a memory. In all cases, however, readers will hopefully learn something.

Honest efforts were made to find the copyright owners of these photographs. Please contact the authors if you feel we have unfairly used your photograph.

INTRODUCTION

The history of Parkersburg, West Virginia, is as winding as the rivers on which the city resides. An examination of Parkersburg history reveals a microcosm of cultures and people of the nation. Two rivers, the Ohio and the Little Kanawha, still carry names from the first native settlers to the area. Native Americans controlled the area for much of its early history. The Parkersburg area served as a lush hunting ground for many tribes, due to the abundance of wildlife and edible flora.

Europeans first reached the area in the mid-1700s and settlement increased in the area after the Revolutionary War. Capt. Alexander Parker purchased the land at what is now present-day Parkersburg for future use. Capt. James Neal surveyed and built the area's first defenses and a permanent white settlement in 1785, because Native American attacks were common in this era.

The rest of the 18th century was a period of slow but steady growth for the town named for Captain Parker. Parkersburg became a river town, sharing that distinction with its upriver neighbor Marietta, Ohio. In 1799, the people of Parkersburg were instrumental in the creation of Wood County, named for Virginia governor James Wood. Parkersburg remains the county seat today. The area also welcomed one of its most infamous residents in 1798: Harman Blennerhassett, who gained notoriety for allegedly funding Aaron Burr's conspiracy concerning western land.

The 19th century was a period of growth for the town. Parkersburg, like much of the United States, benefitted from the various forms of new technology created around the time. The steam engine brought many of those early changes, which drove the local economy by making jobs much easier and faster. Steam-driven boats also carried goods up and down the rivers and established a reliance on the rivers for goods and services. People flooded into the area not only for the available work but also for the entertainments provided by the city. Steam technology also contributed to the development of rail travel. With the arrival of the first railroad line in 1857, Parkersburg became known as a railroad town as much as it had been a river town.

During the Civil War, both Union and Confederate sympathies were found in the area. Parkersburg was almost immediately occupied by the Union army due to the importance of controlling the river and rail traffic. The area served as a staging area and hospital for Union troops for the duration of the Civil War. Fort Boreman was eventually built to protect Union interests.

Fort Boreman took its name from the first governor of the newly created state of West Virginia, Arthur Inghram Boreman. Due to the support of the rebellion by Virginia, unionists formed the Reorganized Government of Virginia to care for the affairs of Union-loyal Virginians. The new Virginia government sided with a growing sense of separation in western Virginia, and on June 20, 1863, West Virginia became a state. Parkersburg quickly became one of the most influential areas in the new state.

Arthur I. Boreman presided over the Second Wheeling Convention, which had effectively created the state, and he was a natural choice to lead the new state. He was a lawyer by trade and lived in the city of Parkersburg. Boreman's administration created many of the state's original public works and the public school system. He was hard on Confederates and supported measures to keep Confederate veterans out of public office. Arthur I. Boreman was not the last Parkersburg native to serve as governor of West Virginia.

Governor William Erskine Stevenson, the third governor of West Virginia, was also from Parkersburg. Unlike his predecessor Boreman, Stevenson supported and successfully reinstated the Confederate veterans' right to vote. He kept a house on Juliana Street, and after leaving politics, he began to court with the growing oil and gas industry in the area.

People often think of coal as the main resource in West Virginia, but for Parkersburg it was oil and natural gas. Parkersburg was involved very early in the industry, with some claiming that it predated Drake's Well in Titusville, Pennsylvania. As the oil boom hit, businesses sprang up all over the city to accommodate the industries' growth. Fortunes were made—and made quickly—during this period and it could be argued that this was Parkersburg in its prime. Historic districts like Juliana and Ann Streets were built and mansions resulted from the overflowing coffers of oil and gas money, which quickly began to dot the landscape in Parkersburg. William Henry "Uncle Wig" Bickel was an example of the enormous wealth created, building a stunning mansion with a zoo and fairgrounds that were open to the citizenry.

Parkersburg began to build, and Romanesque structures like the city building and the Wood County courthouse became part of the Parkersburg skyline as the city moved into the 20th century. Theaters, libraries, dancehalls, sports of all kinds, and saloons all worked to keep Parkersburg entertained. Parkersburg also enjoyed two amusement parks, complete with roller coasters, during this period, as well as its own brewery. These were high times for the city of Parkersburg.

Chemicals also became an important part of the economy. The chemical industry benefitted from the rivers and transportation that the region provided, creating many jobs. However, the city paid a definite environmental cost over the years. The latter half of the 20th century marked a stark decline in Parkersburg and its manufacturing side of the economy. By the end of the 20th century, Parkersburg was in trouble, with the industrial infrastructure that had supported the city long gone.

All good things usually come to an end. Parkersburg's good fortune was no different. Many prominent buildings have been lost due to lack of funds, fire, and misguided attempts to modernize. The local economy has been struggling since those oil boom days. A walk through the city of Parkersburg gives visitors a sense of a "Detroit on the Ohio." The once-vibrant city is now struggling to redefine itself and in the process is losing its history at an alarming rate. All the news is not bad. Parkersburg has continued to push for innovation and has been courting new industry. As the city moves into the 21st century, no one can guess what the future may hold.

One

A GROWING CITY

Until the early 1970s, Market Street was the main shopping district in the city. It hosted a variety of stores, from mom-and-pop businesses to many prominent department stores like Dil's, G.C. Murphy's, and many more. Market Street entered a period of decline as a shopping district after the development of the Grand Central Mall in the neighboring town of Vienna in 1972. (Courtesy of Brian Kesterson.)

One of the more famous structures in early Parkersburg was the home of Harman and Margaret Blennerhassett. Completed in 1800, the Blennerhassetts lived in the mansion until it burned in 1811, often hosting members of the Burr Conspiracy. The current mansion is a reconstruction. (Courtesy of Blennerhassett Island Historical State Park.)

The Cook House was built in 1829 by the Cook family. It is the oldest brick home still located in its original location, on Murdoch Avenue in Parkersburg. The Junior League of Parkersburg manages the property and opens it for special tours, school field trips, and engagements. (Courtesy of Artcraft Studio.)

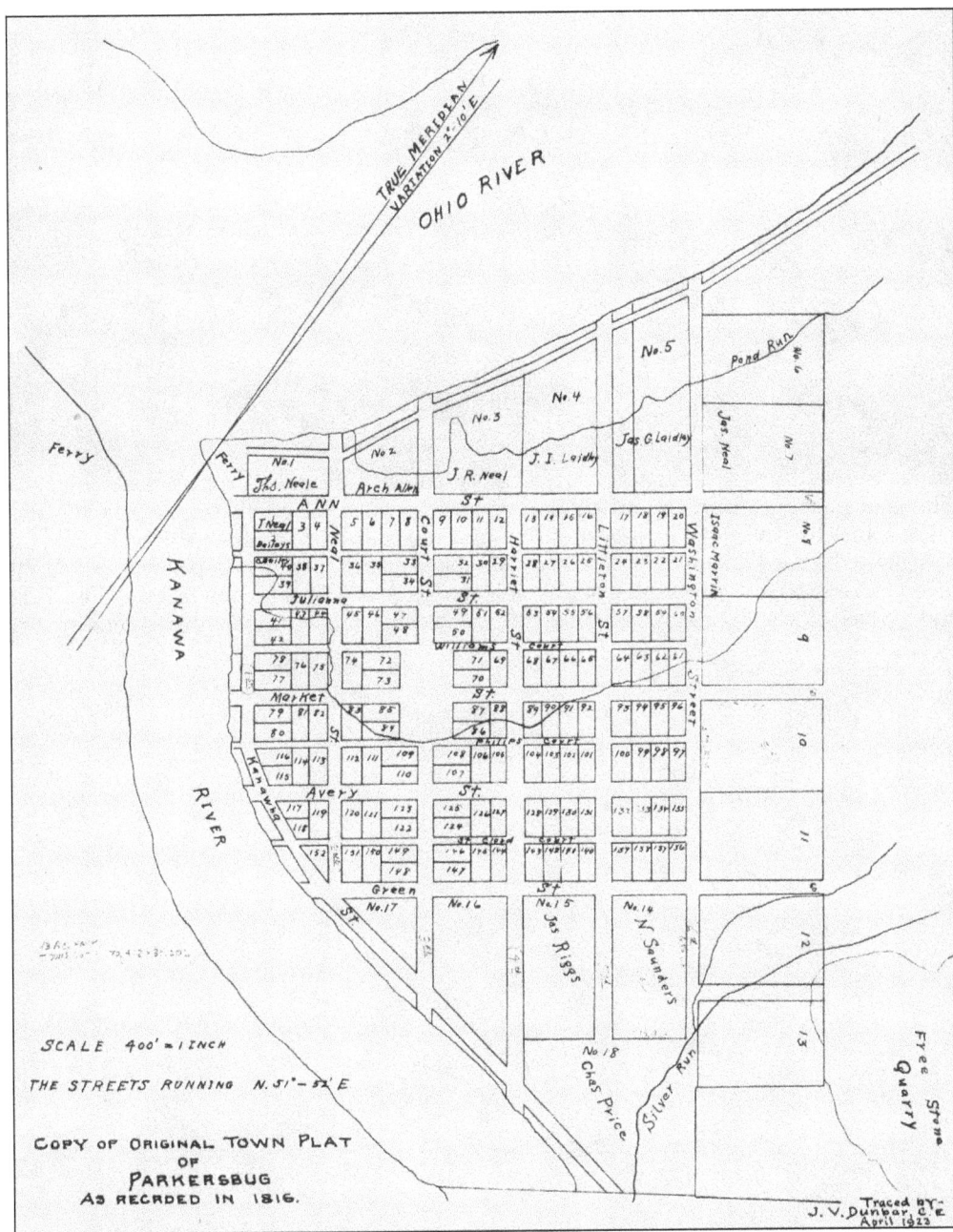

The land occupied by the city of Parkersburg was claimed from Native Americans by Robert Thornton in 1773. In 1783, he sold 1,350 acres to Alexander Parker, for whom the city is named. This original claim was settled and eventually incorporated as Newport by the state of Virginia in 1800. Descendants of Parker, however, were not satisfied with the town's name and contested the designation. Virginia's general assembly relented and renamed the town Parkersburg in 1810. As this 1823 copy of the 1816 map of the town indicates, Parkersburg was a community barely removed from the frontier. The town extended only six blocks from the confluence of the Ohio and Little Kanawha Rivers. Given time to grow, the city, like the Union itself, would not be recognizable by the end of the century. (Courtesy of the City of Parkersburg.)

This panorama of Parkersburg in 1909 shows a city nestled at the confluence of the Ohio and Little Kanawha Rivers but cannot show the excitement that the Industrial Revolution had brought to the mid-Ohio River Valley. In a 1907 compendium of economic, political, and social life in Parkersburg, the city boasted of what it had become and what the future could hold. First and foremost, the city leaders emphasized that Parkersburg, in a little more than a century, was

a modern city with "fifteen miles of brick-paved streets, twenty miles of electric street railways, good sewerage, good water and light systems, splendid schools . . . and many advantages of a city even larger than this." The city also boasted 10 banks and about 200 industrial facilities. The city was prosperous, and the future looked bright. (Courtesy of the Library of Congress.)

Views from Fort Boreman Hill are breathtaking. The fort never saw combat, but was used in conjunction with the Pest House for the treatment of disease and was an important watch post for river and rail traffic during the Civil War. Fort Boreman began to fall into disarray until local historians and politicians took renewed interest in the area as a state park, turning it into a state historical park featuring walking trails and picnic tables. It was opened to the public as a Civil War park in 2007. (Above, courtesy of Brian Kesterson; below, courtesy of Aaron Crites.)

The Parkersburg City Building was built in the Romanesque style at the corner of Fifth and Market Streets. The grand clock tower sported a clock commissioned for purchase by J. Wetherell & Son, a well-known jeweler in town whose own store clock now stands outside the new municipal building. The city building was a staple of the Parkersburg skyline for many years, but it was not large enough to handle all of the services that the citizenry needed it to. Despite a heated campaign to save the building, it was unceremoniously razed while under protest in 1980. (Courtesy of Artcraft Studio.)

River improvements were needed for the livelihood of Parkersburg. At the beginning of the 20th century, federal funds paid for the construction of several locks and dams around Parkersburg. One below Parkersburg created a deep pool in the river for Parkersburg Harbor. Appropriations were made for a lock and dam on the Muskingum River to carry ore from the Great Lakes to West Virginia's coal. (Courtesy of Brian Kesterson.)

Blennerhassett Island was not always a state park, as it is shown here. The land was privately owned and used for a variety of activities, both legal and illegal. Residents farmed the land and the island was used for social activities such as baseball games and picnics. Legend also has it that Blennerhassett was used for bootlegging and moonshining. The island became a historical state park in 1980. (Courtesy of Artcraft Studio.)

In the early days of the Parkersburg Fire Department, horses were an essential part of the firefighting team. The pros and cons of the use of horses by fire departments were debated through the end of the 19th century. Although an integral contributor to the department's success, their maintenance was also an expense to the city. Like the firefighters themselves, the horses needed to be fed—and it was not free. This 1905 bill and city invoice showed the city owed Henry C. Jackson Company of Parkersburg $8.06 for straw. A different kind of cost emerged in the 1920s as the city modernized with fire trucks. (Courtesy of the PFD.)

Parkersburg, W. Va., *Sept 14th* 1905

M City Fire Department

To DR. J. G. GALLANDER, Dr.

OFFICE TELEPHONE 921   VETERINARY SURGEON.   RESIDENCE TELEPHONE 2-1.

Honorary Graduate Ontario Veterinary College.

Residence and Office, 921 Ann Street.—Both Phones.

The fire horses, like most athletes, were chosen for their physical skills; they had to be strong, fast, and healthy. After a three-month training period, new horses were added to the department's stable. But training did not stop there—every day at noon, the department practiced around city hall, usually with a large crowd watching the racing horses and fire wagon. In order for the horses to remain reliable and at their peak, they had to receive regular care provided by a veterinarian. This bill and invoice from Dr. J.G. Gallagher for $19.75 shows that this was also not free. City hall moved rather slowly to pay the vet, taking more than two months, while paying for the straw only four days after being billed. (Courtesy of the PFD.)

Form No. 6.

Parkersburg, W. Va. *June 23* 1905

The City of Parkersburg,

To   *Dr J.C. Callander*   Dr.

For:—   *Bill att'd*   19 75

The above obligation has been properly incurred and the amount is a proper charge against *O & M* appropriation for the *Fire* Department for the year 190 *5*   *Frank Good* Auditor.

The above obligation has been made pursuant to an order of the Board of Affairs at a meeting held on *June 22 1905*   President B. of A.

Payment approved.   Mayor.

Received *July 23rd* 19.5 , $ *19 75* in full of the above account.

Please date, sign and return this voucher. If amount is not correct, return all papers for correction.

18

Firefighting is inherently dangerous work—sometimes just getting to the fire is dangerous. On December 9, 1970, a PFD truck driven by Billy Gene Scott crashed with Carl D. Dodrill's 1966 Buick at the intersection of Spring and Sixteenth Streets. Dodrill's wife, Connie, and son, Carl, were taken to a hospital for head injuries and lacerations. Firefighters on the truck were evaluated, but they were deemed not seriously injured and released. Both vehicles were extensively damaged. The Dodrills' Buick suffered $1,200 dollars of damage and the fire truck, with $15,000 in damages, was so severely damaged that it was taken out of service. (Both, photographs by Harry Barnett; courtesy of the Harry Barnett family from the collection of the PFD.)

Creation of a city fire department was another important step in the modernization of Parkersburg. The city council appointed the first fire chief, John Barrows, in 1889, and eventually provided him with a professional fire department in 1897 to replace the volunteer corps. As a river city, along with their regular firefighting duties, Parkersburg firefighters are also responsible for performing water rescues and recoveries. Over the years, the city operated rescue craft such as this one, acquired by Wood County Emergency Services in the early 1970s for use by first responders in the various local communities. (Courtesy of the PFD.)

Parkersburg has adopted new media whenever it becomes available. The first local newspaper, the *Parkersburg Republican*, was founded in 1833 and was followed by many others, including the current *Parkersburg News and Sentinel*. The city's first radio station, WPAR, was founded in 1935. Another important step forward for Parkersburg was the creation of the first local television station, WTAP, in 1953. The first person to appear live on a WTAP broadcast was Tom Neale. One of the first popular and enduring local TV personalities was sports anchor Sam Slater, seen here, who was known for his enthusiasm and his love of pets. Part of his sports report included news of lost pets, which people believed was an actual segment, not something Slater had included on his own. Long after Slater was gone, people still called to put their pet on the air. Slater also had an unwitting ability to mispronounce names. (Courtesy of Artcraft Studio.)

Two

BUSINESS AND INDUSTRY

As with most of West Virginia, Parkersburg benefited from and was shaped by the extractive industries. Oil and natural gas were an important part of the city's wealth. Evidence of the impact of these industries is seen in images like this one, showing a couple of oil wells on the outskirts of Parkersburg near the neighboring area of Mineral Wells. Evidence of the oil boom can still be seen today and the area is beginning to experience a revival of this industry, with more lucrative oil and gas prices. (Courtesy of Brian Kesterson.)

Early drilling methods were extremely dangerous. Independent oil producers, known as Wildcatters, used explosives and crude early drilling technologies to get to the "liquid gold," but it was not a guaranteed venture. Many fortunes were made and lost around Parkersburg. Eventually, the area's rich resources drew the attention and interest of major companies such as Standard Oil and the Cabot Corporation. The local well pictured here has managed to show oil and has the possibility to be a producer. Wells like this one were responsible for the development of area businesses and the mansions through much of Parkersburg, particularly in the Ann Street area of the city. (Courtesy of Brian Kesterson.)

William Henry "Wig" Bickel was perhaps one of the most important of the independent oil and gas men in Parkersburg, amassing a sizable fortune from his uncanny ability to locate pockets of oil and gas in Wood, Wirt, and Calhoun Counties. He was an avid horseman and received national attention for his trick performing horses. "Uncle Wig" had a mansion constructed with hand-painted murals of prominent local landmarks on the interior. The bricks were hand-cut by Italian stonemasons who Bickel brought to America. It included water features, statues, and copper water spouts. The property also had a working gas well. (Courtesy of Artcraft Studio.)

The county's fifth courthouse, which is still in use, was built between 1899 and 1901 by Caldwell and Drake, at a price tag of $100,000—over $2.5 million today. Designed with modified Richardsonian Romanesque architecture, it included local sandstone, oak woodwork, a marble fountain, and a bust of former state circuit judge James Monroe Jackson. The Wood County Courthouse is one of the few city buildings from the Victorian era to survive into the 21st century. The efforts of local preservation activists in the early 1980s saved the building from the wrecking ball after it had fallen into disrepair. The needed renovations were completed in 1984 at a cost of $1.5 million—more than $3 million today. The courthouse was added to the National Register of Historic Places in 1979. (Courtesy of the Library of Congress.)

Just like any other city, Parkersburg has had its vices. The Rapp and Hebrank Lager Beer Brewery was the premier brewery for the city of Parkersburg and the surrounding areas. It was originally located on Marrtown Road (above) on the south side of Parkersburg but it could not meet the city's thirst requirements, so the family-owned brewery relocated to a bigger brewery on 648 Seventh Street (below). After the move, it was renamed the Parkersburg Brewing Company. The new building stood empty for many years after the brewery closed due to competition from larger brewers. (Both, courtesy of Artcraft Studio.)

The Commercial Banking and Trust Company opened on November 17, 1903, focusing on business loans and individual savings accounts. The bank held approximately $200,000 in savings by 1907. The bank's vice president and cashiers were members of the Wetherell family, who were prominent jewelers in the Parkersburg area. Parkersburg was also the location for many different manufacturing plants during its industrial peak. Among the larger employers were Textron, a manufacturer of machine tools, which was also known as Fastenal and Walker Machine Works. Like many local employers, Textron eventually moved out of Parkersburg to Williamstown and finally closed its plant in 2004. (Courtesy of Brian Kesterson.)

The Storck Baking Company, run by Louis Storck in north Parkersburg, was the main bakery for the Parkersburg area from 1919 until 1975. The building stood empty for years but was converted into the Nip N' Cue pool hall and dance club in the 1990s. (Courtesy of Artcraft Studio.)

The Ames Shovel Plant was a manufacturing staple in Parkersburg until 2005. The company was one of America's oldest businesses, starting in Massachusetts in 1775. Ames purchased an existing business and opened the Parkersburg branch in 1931, and the branch quickly became the home office. The plant was sold to TruTemper in 1999 and was closed due to contract disputes with the United Steelworkers Union. (Courtesy of Artcraft Studio.)

Much of the area's manufacturing was converted to help with the war effort in World War II. The Ames Shovel Plant was used for the production of military goods, making military-grade shovels and tools, tank plating, and aircraft fuel tanks like these. After the war ended, Ames returned to its normal production. (Courtesy of Artcraft Studio.)

The Corning Glass Works Parkersburg facility was built in 1942 with funding from the US government during World War II. The factory built optical glassware for bombsights, telescopes, photographic equipment, and other things during the war. These photographs show employees molding glass and inspecting products for quality control. After the war, Corning reached an agreement with the War Assets Corporation to purchase the property in 1946. Corning eventually used the plant to manufacture glass tubing. In 1994, the facility was sold to SCHOTT Scientific Glass, which closed it in 2004. (Both, courtesy of the Library of Congress.)

Three

DAILY LIFE

Andrew Carnegie was a wealthy steel industrialist who gave back to communities by building libraries and halls for the arts. The Parkersburg Carnegie Library was built in 1905. Stained-glass windows and a wrought-iron spiral staircase were just a few of the major features. The building was most recently the Trans-Allegheny Bookstore until the owner's death. It is currently closed to the public. (Courtesy of Artcraft Studio.)

The Carnegie Library was eventually used as both part of the Parkersburg High School and the board of education until community needs forced the building of a larger city school. Built in the Tudor style of architecture, the Parkersburg High School (PHS) building, seen here in a similar configuration to how it looks today, was first opened in 1917. The school eventually built a gymnasium, stadium, and planetarium. It remains one of the largest campuses in the state. A second high school was built in Parkersburg only after there was a graduating class of almost 1,200 students in 1965, and the area's deepest rivalry was created. (Above, courtesy of Artcraft Studio; below, courtesy of Robert Anderson.)

As the student population at PHS continued to increase, a decision was made in 1965 to build another high school in Parkersburg. Franklin Junior High School, which had been a feeder school for PHS, was closed as a junior high and later reopened as the second high school in Parkersburg. Parkersburg South High School (PSHS) was housed in the original Franklin Junior High Building and is the chief rival to the original Parkersburg High School, with the school's annual football games still bringing in huge crowds. Parkersburg South remained relatively untouched until the development of the Erickson All Sports Facility in 1993 and more renovations in 2005. (Courtesy of Aaron Crites.)

Parkersburg, like the entire state, was segregated, with African American children not permitted to attend school with white children. Despite the racial discrimination, African American community leaders established Sumner School, which remained in use until the Civil Rights Movement of the 1950s began the process of ending segregation in the United States. Sumner School provided an educational opportunity for African American children and represented the will of the people. The school also represented two firsts. Established in 1862 and named after abolitionist politician Charles Sumner of Massachusetts, it was the first free school in West Virginia, made so by wealthy African Americans, who pooled their resources so the children could attend for free. Sumner School was also the first African American school south of the Mason-Dixon Line. In 1866, the city brought Sumner School under the authority of the local board of education. (Courtesy of Artcraft Studio.)

In the early 1960s, Parkersburg's leaders determined that residents wanted and needed local access to affordable higher education for the community's continued growth. Their goal, with the cooperation of the state, was realized with the founding of the Parkersburg branch of West Virginia University in 1961. The original campus consisted of the abandoned Emerson Elementary School and an adjacent Quonset hut on Emerson Avenue. From the first class of 104 students, the college continued to expand and outgrew the original space. Other local organizations used the facilities as well. Along with size, suitability seemed to be an issue as well, with critics claiming that the Quonset hut was unreasonably hot in the summer. The original buildings no longer exist and the original site is now the location of the Parkersburg–Wood County Public Library. (Courtesy of Dennis Bell and WVU at Parkersburg.)

At this crossroads in the school's history, local leaders once again stepped in and supported the construction of a new building. With leaders like former BB&T president Charles Casto behind the bond issue to raise the necessary funds, ground was broken on Staunton Avenue for a new building in 1967, and it was dedicated in 1969. Over the years, space demands required additions to the original building. The college's partnership with the community was strengthened further in 1999 with the opening of the campus's Caperton Center, which offers programs for Wood County high school students to develop workforce skills. (Above, photograph by Harry Barnett, courtesy of the Harry Barnett family from the collection of WVU at Parkersburg; below, courtesy of Dennis Bell and WVU at Parkersburg.)

DeSales Heights Academy was a unique educational opportunity in Parkersburg. The Sisters of the Visitation of Holy Mary, a cloistered teaching order, established the school in 1902 as a boarding school for young women, although some students commuted. The sisters first arrived in Parkersburg in 1864 and ran a school for the city's poor. In 1900, they acquired land on Garfield Avenue and ran their boarding school for 75 years. They replaced the academy in 1977 with the state's first Montessori school. The sisters closed the school in 1992 when enrollment declined and maintenance became too costly. Vandalism and a fire led to the decision to raze the building in 2002. The DeSales Heights building also served as a convent for the nuns. Although un-cloistered as teachers, the Sisters of Visitation resumed their cloistered lives after school. (Both, courtesy of Artcraft Studio from the collection of Kitty Brown.)

The well-respected academics of DeSales required the Sisters to teach a broad curriculum. As these photographs indicate, the school's curriculum included a core education, such as science, in what is now a quite dated laboratory. Students attested that at the time of the photograph, the lab was indeed up-to-date and fully functioning. The sisters also taught the young women skills they needed for employment. In an era when women were usually employed only as teachers, nurses, or secretaries, emphasis was placed there. The commercial room, with the girls in front of typewriters and shorthand notepads, was used for that purpose. (Both, courtesy of Artcraft Studio from the collection of Kitty Brown.)

In this photograph, DeSales students play tennis and volleyball in what appears to be a gym class. The sisters emphasized physical fitness as part of an education. Notice the high wooden fence encircling the DeSales campus. (Courtesy of Artcraft Studio from the collection of Kitty Brown.)

Many young women from across the state and some international students lived at the school. Thus, the young women waving in this photograph were literally saying goodbye as they moved on in life. In this bittersweet moment made lighter by mugging for the camera, the girls part with their high school youth and move into adulthood. (Courtesy of Artcraft Studio from the collection of Kitty Brown.)

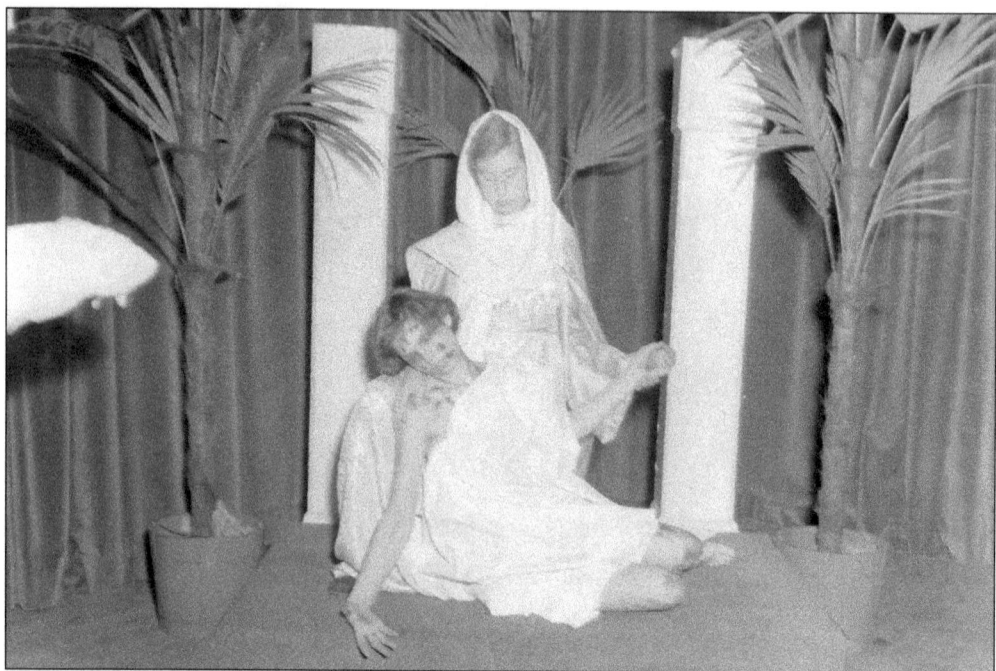

One of the school's requirements was participation in a fall and spring play. In these photographs, the girls perform the *Passion of Christ*. Because it was a girls' boarding school, boys were strictly forbidden from these activities. However, when animals were needed, they were used, like when a donkey was once used for a performance of the *Christmas Story*. Although this was a Catholic school and religion was central to the education and activities, religious themes were not necessary for their plays. (Both, courtesy of Artcraft Studio from the collection of Kitty Brown.)

Members of the segregated Parkersburg Baptist Church formed Zion Baptist in 1866, and it has been influential in the community since. In 1944, a chapter of the National Association for the Advancement of Colored People was formed there. In 1968, Rev. Preston Smith, the pastor of Zion Baptist, was the first African American elected to the Parkersburg City Council. (Courtesy of Artcraft Studio.)

Parkersburg has had a strong Roman Catholic population from the city's very early years. The large numbers necessitated a larger facility in the 1860s, and the current St. Francis Xavier Roman Catholic Church—"St. X" to locals—was built. Construction was completed in 1870 at a cost of $60,000. The church has been restored several times and St. X was added to the National Register of Historic Places in 1978. (Courtesy of Aaron Crites.)

Founded by Parkersburg's Roman Catholic community in 1901, the Parkersburg Knights of Columbus was one of many local fraternal organizations created during a rush in the late 1800s and early 1900s. Without a facility of their own, the Knights met in a local bank until the mid-1920s, when they purchased and refurbished this house on Market Street. Over the next 30 years, the Knights periodically enlarged their facility for their meetings and functions. Increasing membership and the popularity of their social gatherings demanded a larger facility, so they razed this building in the 1950s and built their current facility. The current building has since been enlarged and renovated several times since it was first built. Food at the Knights of Columbus has always drawn a diverse crowd, not limited to Roman Catholics. A cross-section of Parkersburg was seen at the Knights hall: rich, poor, reputable, and not so reputable. (Courtesy of Artcraft Studio from the collection of the Knights of Columbus.)

Although not an official part of Parkersburg until 1950, South Parkersburg's history is intertwined with its neighbor across the Little Kanawha River. One of the first service stations in Parkersburg was actually South Parkersburg's Fort Neal Service Station, which advertised full automobile service. (Courtesy of Artcraft Studio.)

The Windmill Quaker State at the corner of Eighth and Ann Streets was designed by George Nichols and Glen Reynolds and built in 1928. First a Sterling Oil service station, it eventually became a Quaker State station. In 1995, the owners turned the building into a restaurant, but later they moved and left the building empty. The structure was listed on the National Register of Historic Places in 1982. (Courtesy of Artcraft Studio.)

Parkersburg did not rely solely on extractive industries, agriculture, and manufacturing. As with all cities, Parkersburg also had a thriving service industry. This truck was a water wagon at the Springdale Ice Plant and was most likely used by one of the many icehouses until refrigeration became commonplace. Icehouses were still present in Parkersburg even into the 1970s. (Courtesy of Brian Kesterson.)

The Oberymeyers are longtime residents of the Parkersburg area and owners of one of the premier floral shops in the city. Seen here is a piece of property the Oberymeyer family was selling. The family was one of many who made Parkersburg their home and whose name became synonymous with city life. (Courtesy of Brian Kesterson.)

Citizens of Parkersburg enjoyed a broad range of activities throughout the years. The city's earlier history harkened back to a simpler time. Here, the Bickel family enjoys a sleigh ride with some of the many family pets, which "Wig" Bickel trained himself. (Courtesy of Artcraft Studio.)

Lois Kesterson is seen here on her new Indian motorcycle. The fact that a woman was riding a motorcycle in that era is odd, but so is the fact that she is wearing pants. Parkersburg, like much of West Virginia, was slow to embrace fashion, but seemed to abandon those conservative ideals sometimes for entertainment. (Courtesy of Brian Kesterson.)

Through the fire department's outreach programs, such as fire safety and prevention, the department's influence has been widespread over the years. In 1948, they began a program for school-age children, where children went through department training similar to that received by actual firefighters on preventing fire and responding to a fire crisis. The children who completed the program became junior firefighters. Firefighters also filled other needs in the community, helping their city neighbors in need of necessities by making food baskets for distribution at Christmas. As seen in this photograph, firefighters also had the enjoyable task of decorating the town for Christmas. Their ladder trucks certainly made the job easier, if not safer. The fire department has since relinquished this honor to other city workers. (Courtesy of the PFD.)

Several people, without being famous or having their names on streets or buildings, have been influential in the community. Vincent "Jimmy" Borrelli—not even his son knows why he was called Jimmy—had an interest in photography and started Artcraft Studio in 1925 as a self-taught photographer. With his keen eye, Borrelli not only recorded the people and places of a bygone era in Parkersburg, he captured the essence of those people and the culture of the city. His son, Paul, learned photography from his father and continued the legacy of archiving the life of Parkersburg. Many of the images in this book were recorded by Jimmy and Paul Borrelli. (Courtesy of Artcraft Studio.)

Bill Hendricks was another individual with Parkersburg connections who had a national impact, working at the Smoot Theater before relocating to Los Angeles. After World War II, Maj. Bill Hendricks, United States Marine Corps Reserves, expanded his wife's idea to provide toys for needy children. He and other Los Angeles–area Marine reservists collected and distributed toys for Christmas 1947, after which Toys for Tots became an event owned by the Marine Corps. (Courtesy of Artcraft Studio.)

William Peyton lived a remarkable life, living to the incredible age of 127 after coming to Parkersburg as a slave of George Creel. Born in 1792, when George Washington was president, he died in 1919, during Woodrow Wilson's second term. After his emancipation, he relocated to Ohio but regularly returned to visit. Although there is not conclusive evidence, this image may show Peyton on the left. (Courtesy of Bill and Nordeen Yearego.)

Four

POLITICS AND WAR

Arthur I. Boreman served as West Virginia's first governor, from 1863 to 1869. Born in Waynesburg, Pennsylvania, in 1823 and raised in Tyler County, Boreman relocated to Parkersburg in 1846, serving in the Virginia legislature between 1855 and 1861. As a committed Unionist, Boreman supported statehood for western Virginia and was elected as the state's first governor. (Courtesy of the Library of Congress.)

Gen. Thomas "Stonewall" Jackson was originally from the Clarksburg area, but visited and passed through Parkersburg on his way through Virginia. He is considered to be one of the greatest Confederate generals of the Civil War. During the war, he harassed the town and was sighted around the Mineral Wells area. His family went on to a level of political prominence in the city of Parkersburg, serving in a variety of capacities. General Jackson never got the chance to return to the area after the war, as he was accidently shot by his own men in 1863 at Chancellorsville and had his arm amputated, later dying from disease in his weakened state. (Courtesy of Brian Kesterson.)

Gen. George B. McClellan (right and below) was the Union general primarily responsible for the early campaigns in western Virginia. His invasion into the area arguably opened the door for the creation of the state, but he was more concerned with keeping river and rail traffic open for the war effort. He visited the city of Parkersburg at the beginning of the war, but there are no known photographs of that visit. General McClellan was an excellent logistics man but had a lackluster career in the Civil War and was eventually removed by Pres. Abraham Lincoln for having a "case of the slows," a reference to McClellan's propensity to over-train and prepare for battle. (Both, courtesy of Brian Kesterson.)

Bvt. Maj. Gen. Thomas Maley Harris was originally from the Harrisville area and was a doctor by trade. He was partially responsible for the recruitment of the 10th West Virginia Infantry during the Civil War. General Harris also served on the commission that tried the Abraham Lincoln conspirators, but left the Union army in 1866. He lived to be 90 years old and passed on in 1906. (Courtesy of Brian Kesterson.)

Gen. William Woods Averell was a Union general responsible for leading the West Virginia Cavalry during the Civil War. He fought at the Battle of Droop Mountain among many other engagements in West Virginia. An avid inventor, General Averell is credited with the invention of asphalt and also had numerous other patents for inventions throughout his life. (Courtesy of Brian Kesterson.)

Parkersburg's location on river and rail transportation routes made it an important military objective at the start of the Civil War. The 14th Ohio regiment, under the command of Colonel James B. Steedman, crossed the Ohio River from Marietta, Ohio, on the morning of Monday, May 27, 1861, beginning around 7:00 am. By midnight, they had occupied Parkersburg, and the city remained under Union control for the remainder of the war. (Courtesy of Artcraft Studio.)

George Harwood Bailey, from the Lubeck area, was a prominent farmer in the region his entire life, gaining notoriety in the Parkersburg area for being a Confederate spy. His story is a good example of the torn loyalties of locals during the Civil War. Parkersburg was under the control of Union troops for most of the war due to the importance of the river and rail travel, but many residents of Parkersburg gathered information for the Confederacy because their loyalties did not lie with the Union. West Virginia was truly a border state during the Civil War, which created a lot of tension among the residents. (Courtesy of Brian Kesterson.)

Parkersburg saw a resurgence of the Ku Klux Klan in the 1920s. This 1934 photograph shows a long line of KKK marchers in Parkersburg during one particular demonstration. The KKK targeted African Americans as well as recent immigrants, Roman Catholics, Jews, and anyone they deemed to be acting inappropriately. (Courtesy of Artcraft Studio.)

Located on Seventh Street in Parkersburg, the Stephenson House was originally James M. Stephenson's home on his Oakland Plantation. Slave labor and craftsmen built this Greek Revival style house around 1840. Stephenson was a lawyer, a one-term member of the Virginia General Assembly, and the president of Parkersburg National Bank. The building was added to the National Register of Historic Places in 1979. (Courtesy of the Library of Congress.)

The Arthur Ingraham Boreman house, home of the first governor of West Virginia, was on the corner of Fourth and Avery Streets. While he lived in Parkersburg, Boreman practiced law. He was selected as governor on June 20, 1863, serving two terms and eventually becoming a senator. He returned to his Parkersburg home to practice law but was elected as a circuit court judge in 1888. Boreman died at his home in 1896 and is interred in the Odd Fellow's Cemetery behind Parkersburg High School. The house was demolished and is currently a parking lot, marked only by a small stone designating the site. (Courtesy of Artcraft Studio.)

Parkersburg native Cpl. Joseph E. Turner prepares to ship out to Paris with the American Expeditionary Force to fight in World War I in 1918. Corporal Turner most likely saw action in France during the Aisne Offensive. Notice the horse carriage—while automobiles were available, many residents still relied on older means of transportation. (Courtesy of Brian Kesterson.)

World War II was fought in faraway, exotic places. In 1943, to raise money for the war effort, the War Department sent this captured Japanese two-man submarine to American cities. The sale of war bonds from this promotion raised millions of dollars. (Courtesy of Artcraft Studios.)

John Jay Jackson Sr. was a Parkersburg native and the sire of one of the most influential political families in West Virginia. His son was federal district judge John Jay Jackson Jr., also of Parkersburg, who is immortalized in statue form outside of the Wood County Courthouse. Another son, James Monroe Jackson, became a circuit judge, and another, Jacob Beeson Jackson, became the sixth governor of West Virginia. Jackson Sr. was also partly responsible for the construction of Trinity Episcopal Church and was an avid supporter of the temperance movement. He passed away in 1877. The Jackson Memorial Fountain at the entrance to the City Park in Parkersburg is also dedicated to the Jackson family. (Courtesy of Brian Kesterson.)

The Camden House, at 717 Ann Street, was the home of Johnson Newlon Camden. Camden was the right-hand-man of John D. Rockefeller, for whom he controlled petroleum production in West Virginia for much of his life. Camden ran for governor in 1868 but lost. In 1881, he ran for the senate and won, serving until 1887. He would later serve again to fill a vacant seat from 1893 to 1895. Camden died in 1908 and his family donated his home in Parkersburg for use as a city hospital. The house required renovation to be used as a hospital and opened in 1920 with the help of Dr. Andrew Clark. The original structure was eventually demolished to allow for upgrading of the facilities at what became Camden-Clark Memorial Hospital. (Courtesy of Artcraft Studio.)

Pres. William Howard Taft failed to make an impact on the people of Parkersburg after twice traveling through the city. In May 1910, Taft stopped temporarily in Parkersburg on his way from Marietta, Ohio, to the White House and consented to make a few remarks. His crowd totaled about 100 people, although most were, according to the *Parkersburg Sentinel*, "those who generally gather at the station in the evenings and some others who were attracted by the coming of the president." City leaders also failed to attend. When given another chance in June, the city intended to impress Taft, who again was to make a stop while traveling to and from Marietta. While 2,000 people attended, they showed little spirit for the president. This photograph is from Taft's arrival in Marietta. (Courtesy of Artcraft Studio.)

Pres. Harry S. Truman took his opportunity to speak to the people of Parkersburg while traveling to Bolivar, Missouri, with Venezuelan president Romulo Gallegos to dedicate a statue of Simon Bolivar over the Independence Day weekend of 1948. President Truman appeared before a large crowd during the whistle stop in Parkersburg and, in a short speech, hoped that the new United Nations could achieve the kind of peace for the rest of the world that was already enjoyed in the western hemisphere. His words came during the early days of the Berlin Blockade, when the people of the world were holding their collective breath in fear of World War III. (Courtesy of the Harry S. Truman Library and Museum.)

One of the more important presidential visits to the Parkersburg area was that of Pres. John F. Kennedy, who won the election of 1960 thanks in part to the votes he received in West Virginia. He is seen here in the city park with his brother, Ted Kennedy, who went on to a successful career as an influential senator from Massachusetts. President Kennedy took a great interest in the region and in the state of West Virginia because of the poverty issues that plagued the state. His visit set the tone for the development of the War on Poverty, and later, Pres. Lyndon B. Johnson's Great Society program. (Courtesy of Artcraft Studio.)

Pres. Richard Nixon (right) campaigned in West Virginia but lost the state and the election to John F. Kennedy in 1960. Nixon is seen here speaking in front of the Wood County Courthouse in Parkersburg. Hubert Humphrey, seen below speaking in Parkersburg during the campaign, lost his party's nomination to President Kennedy despite campaigning in West Virginia. Humphrey campaigned again during the 1968 presidential election, which he lost to Nixon. (Both, courtesy of Artcraft Studio.)

Former first lady Barbara Bush stopped in Parkersburg to campaign for her son George W. Bush just days before the memorable and controversial 2000 presidential election. She spoke to a large crowd at Huffman Truss on Old St. Marys Pike, just outside of Parkersburg. Bush (at left) was photographed greeting local resident Floretta Long. Below, then-governor Cecil Underwood spoke to Long with Barbara Bush in the background. Governor Underwood has the unique distinction of being both the youngest and the oldest governor in the state's history—he was first elected in 1956 and again in 1996. (Both, courtesy of Kim Meredith.)

Pres. George W. Bush campaigned heavily in the area during the 2000 and 2004 presidential elections. West Virginia's five electoral votes proved to be deciding factors in Bush's winning the 2000 presidential election. The election was so close that it was contested in numerous states, but West Virginia was carried by Bush. The result remains contested to this day because of its closeness and the fact that Al Gore received more overall votes but lost the election through the Electoral College. (Courtesy of Dennis Bell and WVU at Parkersburg and Aaron Crites.)

Pres. George W. Bush spoke directly to the people of Parkersburg during the 2004 election. Despite security concerns regarding terrorism after September 11, 2001, President Bush spoke to a packed Stadium Field at Parkersburg High School. The event was protested heavily due to concerns over the wars in Iraq and Afghanistan. Despite the protests, President Bush carried the state again in the 2004 presidential election. (Both, courtesy of Aaron Crites.)

Five

ENTERTAINMENT

Camden Theater, at 725 Market Street, was the showpiece of Parkersburg's many movie houses in the early 1900s. With seating for 1,400, the Camden opened as an opera house in the 1890s and began showing movies in the 1910s. In the era of silent movies, live music was important, so Camden installed a pipe organ in 1915 and a newer model in 1925. (Courtesy of Artcraft Studio.)

Of the 11 theaters Parkersburg boasted in the early 1900s, only the Smoot Theater remains. Built originally as a vaudeville hall in 1926, the Smoot was transformed by Warner Brothers into a movie house in 1930, which it remained until it closed in 1986. After standing vacant for three years, the aging and dilapidated structure was set to be destroyed, but volunteers and activists saved it from the wrecking ball by a matter of days in 1989. Through the volunteers' painstaking efforts, the Smoot Theater was returned to its Victorian splendor to remind the city of a different time. The Smoot is seen here after the successful restoration. The Smoot was added to the National Register of Historic Places in 1982. (Courtesy of Aaron Crites.)

The Lincoln Theater (right), across from the Camden Theater at 724 Market Street, opened in 1920 to show silent movies, but converted to "talkies" when they became popular in the late 1920s. The Lincoln closed in 1932 and a department store moved into the site in the mid-1930s. After the store moved out, the Actors Guild of Parkersburg purchased the site. Notice the "likeness" of Abraham Lincoln above the marquee. (Courtesy of Artcraft Studio.)

In a competitive era of movie production and promotion, studios and theaters took great pains to boost attendance. Seen below is a unique local promotion for the Universal Studios film *All Quiet on the Western Front* at the Lincoln Theater. The items on display came from the local American Legion, adding to the authenticity of the display. (Courtesy of Artcraft Studio.)

The Hagenbeck Wallace Circus was the precursor of the Ringling Brothers Circus. Posters like these were placed on buildings throughout town to herald the coming of the circus. The Hagenbeck Wallace Circus was a favorite of "Wig" Bickel, who paid out of his own pocket to bring the circus to town. The Hagenbeck Wallace circus met its end in a train wreck that killed many of their animals and spawned the movie *The Greatest Show on Earth*. The Ringling Brothers (below) also visited Parkersburg and continues to bring the circus to town. (Both, courtesy of Artcraft Studio.)

The opening day parade at the racetrack on the grounds of William Henry "Uncle Wig" Bickel's estate is seen here. Bickel not only opened his estate to the public but shaped his estate to provide entertainment for the entire Parkersburg community. The parade is being led by one of Bickel's ranch hands and horse trainers and followed by the Parkersburg High School Big Red marching band. Parades like this one made the estate and Bickel himself very popular. The legendary combat journalist Ernie Pyle even wrote an article about Bickel's horses, and the entire Bickel family participated in numerous parades throughout the nation. (Courtesy of Artcraft Studio.)

The family used the grandstand on the Bickel Estate to hold local fairs and various concerts and social events for the Parkersburg community. One of the biggest events was the Centennial Rodeo, which was organized to celebrate the 100-year anniversary of West Virginia's statehood. (Courtesy of Artcraft Studio.)

BICKELS' BARN DANCE

NOVEMBER 14, 1941

WE HAVE KILLED AN ELK AND HAVE SWEPT THE BARN
AND ARE READY FOR OUR DANCE, "BY DARN,"
NOVEMBER 14TH, IS THE DATE
FROM 9:00 O'CLOCK 'TIL LATE.
BE SURE AND COME AND WEAR OLD RAGS,
THEY'RE MORE APPROPRIATE WITH OUR NAGS.
FROM 10:30 'TIL 11:00 WE'LL BE ON THE AIR,
SO LISTEN IN, IF YOU CAN'T GET THERE,

UNCLE WIG AND AUNT STELL

This invitation was for a barn dance and elk roast hosted by "Uncle Wig" and "Aunt Stell" Bickel on November 14, 1941. Uncle Wig's irrepressible personality and community-minded exuberance were reflected in the invitation's wording. Note that part of the event was to be broadcast by radio, enabling people to listen in to the festivities. (Courtesy of Aaron Crites.)

The racetrack and grandstand on the Bickel Estate were used for many events until the 1960s. The racetrack provided the perfect venue for the West Virginia Centennial, which included bull and bronco riding, music, and food. Unfortunately, "Wig" Bickel passed away in the 1940s and did not get to see the anniversary. The estate was sold shortly after the celebration and the grandstand and racetrack were destroyed to make way for residential development. (Courtesy of Artcraft Studio.)

William Henry "Wig" Bickel had an elk home that allowed the elk to roam freely on the property as part of his personal menagerie. The elk and elk home were common backdrops for pictures of both the family and visitors to the estate, including celebrities from the era. The structure had Elk Home written on the roof, which often led strangers to mistake the estate for the Elk Lodge for the city of Parkersburg. Confused visitors tried to enter the mansion on many occasions due to the mix-up. Bickel slaughtered an elk annually for his elk roast, inviting personal friends of the family and people of note from the area. Senators and governors were often guests at the Bickel functions. (Courtesy of Artcraft Studio.)

The duck pond was another popular area on the grounds. Picnics were common and "Wig" Bickel even trained the ducks to perform tricks. Bickel liked water features and had working fountains on the grounds. The duck pond also served as a swimming area if the need arose. In addition to community functions, Bickel frequently used the estate as a backdrop for fundraising campaigns for political events, war bond drives, and charity events. Bickel was said to have randomly handed out candy to needy local children. The trees around the estate were also decorated with electric lights at Christmas for the public to enjoy. (Courtesy of Artcraft Studio.)

"Wig" Bickel was responsible for the reemergence of sulky racing—similar to chariot racing—in the area, and it proved to be popular. The track was also used by area harness racers and for fairs, horse shows, and other activities of a similar nature. The grounds were later purchased by the Brown family and the racetrack was destroyed to develop the area. (Courtesy of Artcraft Studio.)

The Coliseum, at the corner of Seventh and Green Streets on what is currently Dick Warner's Kia car lot, sported many different functions, but the dancehall was one of the largest in town and was a popular hangout for many Parkersburg citizens, with local and national acts providing music. (Courtesy of Artcraft Studio.)

Guy Lombardo and His Royal Canadians played to a full Coliseum on May 22, 1934. The price of admission, although rather expensive for the era at $3.50 per couple, did not deter his fans, who were eager to hear the immensely popular Lombardo. The performance was sold out for two weeks. (Courtesy of Artcraft Studio.)

Terrapin Park, at 25th Street and St. Mary's Pike, was an incredible place. Around 1900, the Shattuck family added a casino and an auditorium to the park. The auditorium, which had modern equipment for the era, became a venue for many shows and was rumored to hold upwards of 2,000 people. (Courtesy of Christy and Jeff Little.)

Terrapin Park ▲

H. R. POLLACK, Director

PROGRAM

W. D. Reed Presents the "STRATTON PLAYERS" in

THE MATCHMAKER

A Comedy in Three Acts by JERROLD SHEPARD.

CAST OF CHARACTERS

Father Daly ---W. D. Reed
Arnold Leslie, a young mining engineer--------------Milton W. Hyatt
Jim Carter, a wealthy ranch owner-----------------Robert McIntyre
Colonel Fitzhugh Potter of the U. S. A.----------------Harry Leonard
Willie Beekman, a young New Yorker-----------------Robert Clifford
Pierre, a half-breed------------------------------------Gordon Ruffin
Tom Falon, proprietor of Tom's Place-----------------F. J. Markus
Hope Lee, a Chinaman------------------------------Frank Macdonald
Margaret Manning, Jim Carter's ward-----------------Jane Wa e
Dollie, Father Daly's ward-----------------------------Lois Elliott
Mrs. Wellington, a rich widow----------------------Bessie Clafton
Ann, Jim Carter's housekeeper--------------------Crete Chadwick

SYNOPSIS

ACT I—Main street, Boom City, Idaho.
ACT II—The sitting room at Carter's ranch. Two hours later.
ACT III—Interior of Father Daly's cottage. One hour later.

Next MON., TUES., and WEDNES.,—"AMIE OF THE CIRCUS."
Matinee Saturday at 3:00 P. M.

Terrapin Park was a desirable performing venue for many top acts in show business, including vaudeville acts, musical acts, comedies, and dramas. The auditorium could be used for official functions and included areas to host lakeside picnics and cookouts. The lavish scenery and warm atmosphere made the park a Parkersburg staple for many years. The park fell to a disastrous fire in the offseason and, lacking insurance, was forced to close its doors in 1917. (Courtesy of Brian Kesterson.)

Terrapin Park Theatre

H. R. POLLACK, Director

PROGRAM

W. D. Reed Presents the "STRATTON PLAYERS" in

"BEVERLY OF GRAUSTARK"

CAST OF CHARACTERS

Prince Baldos (known as Baldos)	G. W. Ruffin
General Marlaux	Milton W. Hyatt
Captain Qulunox of the Graustark army	Harry Leonard
Lieut. Castro	Robert Clifford
Ravonne	W. D. Reed
Belmark Followers of Prince Danton	Charles Murray
Franz	Robert Clifford
Princess Yetive, ruler of Graustark	Crete Chadwick
Princess Candace, sister of Prince Danton	Lois Elliot
Aunt Fanny, Beverly Calhoun's maid	Edna Gray
Beverly Calhoun, of Washington, U. S. A.	June Ware

SYNOPSIS

ACT 1.—The Rendezvous of Prince Danton.
ACT 2.—Room in the Castle at Edelweiss.
ACT 3.—Exterior of Royal Palace at Edelweiss.
ACT 4.—The same as Act 3.

Next THURSDAY, FRIDAY and SATURDAY—"THE MATCHMAKER"

The United Woolen Mills Co.

ESTABLISHED 1902

ALL SUITS — ALL OVERCOATS **$15** NO MORE NO LESS

MADE TO ORDER   MADE TO FIT

302 Market Street,   Parkersburg, W. Va.

The proprietors of Terrapin Park presented plays that were quite popular at the time. Patrons saw a performance of *Beverly of Graustark*, from the well-received George Barr McCutcheon book of the same name, which was eventually made into a silent film in 1926. Another offering was a play based on Rex Beach's popular *The Barrier*, which was also made into a silent film in 1926 and then a talking film in 1937. (Both, courtesy of Brian Kesterson.)

Terrapin Park Theatre

H. R. POLLACK, Director

PROGRAM

W. D. Reed Presents the "STRATTON PLAYERS" in

"THE BARRIER"

CAST OF CHARACTERS

Captain Burrell, U. S. A.	G. W. Ruffin
John Gale	Robert Clifford
Dan Starke	Milton W. Hyatt
No Creek Lee	W. D. Reed
Poleon Doret	Harry Leonard
Runnion	Robert McIntyre
Corporal Thomas	Robert McIntyre
Alluna	Crete Chadwick
Molly	Lois Elliott
Necia	June Ware

SYNOPSIS

ACT 1.—John Gale's Trading Post. Afternoon.
ACT 2.—The same. One week later.
ACT 3.—Living Room in Gale's House. Night, same day.
ACT 4.—The Barracks. Midnight.

Next MON., TUES., AND WEDNES.—"BEVERLY OF GRAUSTARK."

The United Woolen Mills Co.

ESTABLISHED 1902

ALL SUITS — ALL OVERCOATS **$15** NO MORE NO LESS

MADE TO ORDER   MADE TO FIT

302 Market Street,   Parkersburg, W. Va.

Around 1900, roller coasters were all the rage in America and became staples in many communities. The Dazy Dazier Dip Coaster, seen here, was a wooden roller coaster at Terrapin Park. It was built in 1913 as part of an upgrade to the park facilities that included many other carnival attractions. The rides were a nickel for kids and a dime for adults and were said to have provided a surprisingly wild ride. Other attractions available to patrons were a Ferris wheel, merry-go-round, and carnival-inspired games. Benches rounded out the carnival feel of the park and allowed visitors the chance to sit back and enjoy the carnival. (Courtesy of Artcraft Studio.)

The Queen Toy Spiritual Band, comprised of children with adult leadership, played authentic music on toy instruments. They used the music to accompany their singing of hymns and Negro spirituals in what their advertisement called a "new and most original way." The group appeared at a variety of venues in the early 1900s. Parkersburg was also home to other distinctive bands, like the Italian-American band, formed by a number of leading families in the Parkersburg Italian-American community, including the Borrellis, the Marchis, the Frezzas, and the Brunicardis. They were fixtures in local parades and once participated in a parade before the president in Washington, D.C. Once, according to legend, a horn player chose to follow a woman who had caught his eye instead of the parade route. (Courtesy of Artcraft Studio.)

After several false starts, the effort to establish a YMCA was finally accomplished in 1905, with the dedication of this magnificent four-story building on Eighth Avenue. Among the facilities were a gym, a swimming pool, showers, bowling alleys, and a library. The final cost of the building, considered the best in West Virginia, was $95,000—more than $2 million today. (Courtesy of Artcraft Studio.)

Established in 1902, the Parkersburg Country Club has been a fixture in the community for more than a century. Although it is in neighboring Vienna, the elite from Parkersburg traveled to the nearby rural area for relaxation. This original building, designed by local architect William Howe Patton, burned in 1936 and was replaced soon after. (Courtesy of Artcraft Studio.)

Parkersburg had many saloons and gambling halls in its early years. Saloon culture began to decline with the advancement of the temperance movement and was shut down during Prohibition. The J. Busch Saloon, on the corner of Ann and Neal Streets before the streets of Parkersburg were numbered, was a good representation of an early-1900s saloon. Note the African American patrons posing alongside white patrons for this photograph. Saloons served their patrons, many of whom were workers in local factories, oil fields, or other extractive industries, whiskey and beer from the local breweries. Establishments like this often featured gambling as well. (Courtesy of Artcraft Studio.)

The costumed mascot, Sparky, and a clown firefighter ride on an old fire engine in one of the parades that were such a big part of the community spirit in Parkersburg. The fire department has always been a fixture in these parades, beginning when the department still used horse-drawn wagons. (Courtesy of the PFD.)

One of the oldest landmark local businesses in Parkersburg is the North End Tavern, also known as the NET. Established in 1899 as a local tavern, the NET has remained in the same location, although it has expanded over the years to include a microbrewery. (Artwork by Ken Hillberry; courtesy of the North End Tavern.)

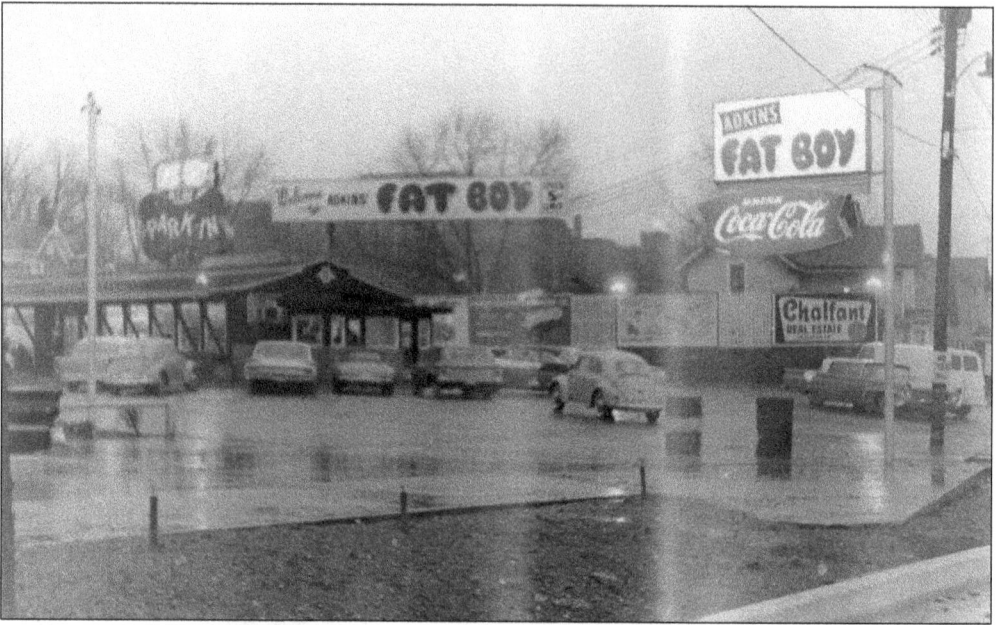

Adkins Fat Boy was a local drive-through and burger joint. During the 1950s and early 1960s, the Fat Boy was a main hangout for area youth. Located at the Parkersburg traffic circle, it was a center point for the local hot-rod culture. (Courtesy of Artcraft Studio.)

Another local restaurant landmark enjoyed by young and old is the Pizza Place. Franco Scotto Rinaldi, seen here tossing pizza dough, started the original mall restaurant with Mike Ruscitto. Scotto Rinaldi, along with his brother, Guiseppe Scotto Rinaldi, and his brother-in-law, Michael Scotto DiLuzio, started two other restaurants in prime locations guaranteed to attract pizza lovers: across from each of the area high schools. (Courtesy of Lisa Ball.)

Six

TRANSPORTATION AND TRAVEL

The Blennerhassett Hotel was built at the corner of Fourth and Market Streets in 1889. Owner Col. William Nelson Chancellor named the hotel for Harman Blennerhassett. It is in the Romanesque design, which allowed it to blend with nearby structures like the city building and the courthouse. The Blennerhassett Hotel still stands and is considered the premier hotel in the area. (Courtesy of Artcraft Studio.)

Col. William N. Chancellor was also involved in the building of another legendary Parkersburg hotel, the Chancellor Hotel. Financed by the Bank Block Investment Company, of which Colonel Chancellor was president, the hotel, at the corner of Market and Seventh Streets, was finished in 1901. It originally had 120 rooms, but 100 more were added in the 1920s. Artwork by locally renowned artist Lily Irene Jackson adorned the walls. Unfortunately, the Chancellor met the same fate as many of the city's early-1900s buildings. The new owner, Union Trust National Bank, had the hotel razed in 1977, but not before the Lily Irene Jackson works were removed and donated to the library. The vacant lot was turned into a parking lot. (Courtesy of Artcraft Studio.)

The Ohio River is extremely important to the city of Parkersburg to this day, providing entertainment and a means to transport goods. Even early in its history, barges transported various goods up and down the river. Shown here is one of the many stern-wheelers from the area that pushed barges past Parkersburg. (Courtesy of Brian Kesterson.)

The stern-wheeler *Tell City* was a common sight around the Parkersburg area. Named after the Ohio River hub of Tell City, Indiana, it was used primarily for passengers until its demise in a 1917 accident. The pilot house was saved and is on display at the Ohio River Museum in neighboring Marietta, Ohio. (Courtesy of Brian Kesterson.)

Although Parkersburg had an obvious transportation route in the Ohio River, the growing town, like so many other communities, wanted and needed the ability to travel overland. After repeated demands from the state's western inhabitants, Virginia relented and built an overland route from Staunton in the Shenandoah Valley to Parkersburg. The Staunton-Parkersburg Turnpike, as it was called, was chartered by the state in 1817, surveyed in 1826, and finally completed in 1847. The Seven Mile House—or the Creel House—seven miles from Parkersburg's center, was one of the many stagecoach stops that serviced travelers along the pike. Even well into the 20th century, the road in the below image was still not paved. (Both, courtesy of Bill and Nordeen Yearego.)

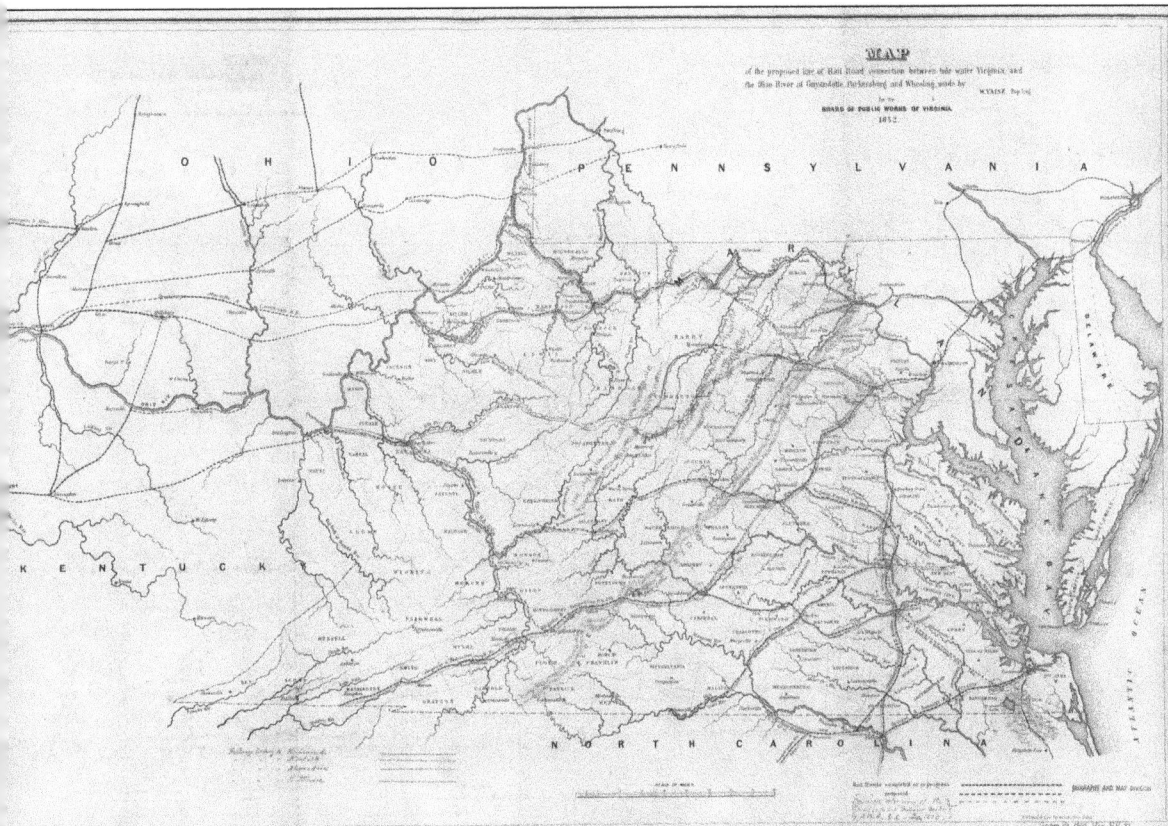

As the United States expanded and the West became increasingly profitable, eastern states competed to control western trade. By the mid-1800s, Virginia had plans to funnel goods through the state's ports. This 1852 map indicates that it also had plans to link the western part of the state with the Tidewater region, with Parkersburg figuring prominently in those plans. When goods were shipped up the Ohio River, Parkersburg would become a port from which the goods could be offloaded to railroads and carried to the Tidewater area and on to other domestic or foreign destinations. Virginia's plans were met, but not quite how it thought. The Baltimore & Ohio (B&O) Railroad ended up connecting Parkersburg with Baltimore instead of the Tidewater area. (Courtesy of the Library of Congress.)

Completed in 1871, the B&O Bridge spans the Ohio River from Parkersburg to Belpre, Ohio. Bridge architect Jacob Linville used new ideas on the bridge, which Andrew Carnegie's Keystone Bridge Company built. The bridge was a significant link in the railroad's mainline from Baltimore to St. Louis. When finished, there were claims that this 7,140-foot bridge was the longest in the world. Even before the bridge was built, Parkersburg was a depot for the railroad, unloading cargo from trains and carrying it across the Ohio River by ferry. From there, the cargo had to be loaded onto the railcars of the Marietta & Cincinnati Railroad. (Left, courtesy of Bill and Nordeen Yearego; below, courtesy of Brian Kesterson.)

3. BELPRE, O - B & O, BRIDGE, FROM PROSPECT HILL - PARKERSBURG - W. VA. FLOOD.

The East Street Bridge was an important link in the development of Parkersburg. The bridge connected Parkersburg with South Parkersburg across the Little Kanawha River. Completed in 1908, the bridge remains in use today as part of East Street and Alternate Route 14. (Courtesy of the Library of Congress.)

Parkersburg's newest bridge, the Blennerhassett Island Bridge, is probably the most controversial bridge in the area. The bridge was part of the Corridor D construction of Route 50 to span the Ohio River from Parkersburg to Belpre, Ohio. Opposition to its location mounted because one of the bridge's piers was to be built on state park land on Blennerhassett Island, but the 4,000-foot bridge was completed in 2008. (Courtesy of Robert Anderson.)

As part of the City of Parkersburg's centennial celebration in 1910, the Wright Brothers were commissioned to perform various aerial feats. The controversial photograph above shows one of the flights over the city. It is believed to be a fake, which was common for shots that needed multiple angles in the early days of still photography. (Courtesy of Artcraft Studio.)

Amelia Earhart (left) visited the area in 1936, flying over the city of Parkersburg as part of a promotion to encourage flying in the area. She landed at the Stewart Air Park, on the grounds of what would become the Grand Central Mall. Five years later, she would disappear attempting to circle the globe. (Courtesy of Artcraft Studio.)

Seven

DISASTERS

*1- House Upside Down,
After Parkersburg, W. Va. Flood.*

One of the unfortunate realities of life in a river city is flooding, and being at the confluence of two rivers increases the likelihood of floods. Parkersburg has experienced its share of devastating floods, with its first major one coming in 1884, followed by one about every quarter-century—in 1913, 1937, and 1950. The 1913 flood was the worst, as floodwaters hit a record stage of 58.9 feet, leaving much of the city underwater and bringing daily life almost to a halt. This photograph of a house turned upside down shows the destructive power of the 1913 flood. (Courtesy of Artcraft Studio.)

The flood dislocated hundreds of residents from their homes and left the downtown under water for days. Refugees without extended families or other accommodations found shelter in the Lyons tabernacle. Basic necessities were provided by local governments and charities. Boy Scouts offered around-the-clock assistance and, thankfully, a feared food shortage never materialized.

To see the relative height of the floodwaters, compare the 1909 panorama of the city on pages 12 and 13 to this panorama, from roughly the same angle across the Little Kanawha River from downtown, during the 1913 flood, using the Mail Pouch wall advertisement (center) as the focal point. (Courtesy of the Library of Congress.)

5. COURT HOUSE & MARKET ST., PARKERSBURG, W. VA. FLOOD. 3-29-13

The 1913 flood that inundated Parkersburg took an even heavier toll on neighboring towns in Ohio and Indiana. The widespread flooding killed more than 400 people, most of whom perished in Ohio, but one of whom died in Parkersburg. City after city faced the same conditions, with raging water bringing city life to a standstill. These images of Market Street show the floodwaters making the main commercial thoroughfare of the city look more like a Venetian canal than a city street. The water covering Market Street reached a depth of more than 20 feet for days before the water receded. (Both, courtesy of Brian Kesterson.)

10. MARKET ST. PARKERSBURG-W. VA. FLOOD, 3-30-13.

The Blennerhassett Hotel is the only early-1900s hotel in the downtown area still in use, despite the efforts of the 1913 flood to wash it away. The hotel, at 320 Market Street, is surrounded by floodwater in this photograph. Although the lower floors were a disaster, the upper floors were safe and allowed the hotel to remain in business. (Courtesy of Brian Kesterson.)

This photograph of the Ohio River Railroad depot at the corner of Ann and Second Streets shows the destructive capacity of the 1913 flood. The depot, with its raised platform and elevated track, survived the flood, but judging from the debris strewn across the ground, many other structures did not. (Courtesy of Brian Kesterson.)

After the 1913 flood, one quarter of the city was under 20 feet of water, including half of the downtown. Businesses were shut down and bars and saloons were ordered to close. To ensure looting did not erupt, troops were brought in to guard the city. Additionally, all overland travel—train, trolley, and pedestrian—came to a halt. The only way to travel was by small boat. Some of the facilities hit by this disaster included the post office and City Hospital (Camden-Clark Hospital). The above image shows that the hospital could be approached only by boat. Below, the first floor of the post office is under water. (Above, courtesy of Bill and Nordeen Yearego; below, courtesy of Brian Kesterson.)

16, SKIRVEN STREET, AFTER PARKERSBURG, W. VA. FLOOD.

Losses caused by the 1913 flood were substantial; the water was estimated to have caused $250,000 in damage. Houses and buildings that were not destroyed were damaged and in need of repair. These photographs, of Skirven—or Skirvin—Street (above) and Twelfth Street (below), show the enormity of the damage in the city. In both photographs, buildings were knocked off their foundations and boards and other debris were jumbled and unrecognizable as part of a finished structure. The residents chose to rebuild the city, which they accomplished, and Parkersburg continued to thrive. (Both, courtesy of Brian Kesterson.)

Ironically, when the floodwaters receded, a major fire erupted out of the soggy conditions of the downtown. Buildings along Ann Street caught fire while the city remained flooded. In this case, water actually contributed to the difficulty of fighting the fire, necessitating the use of boats. (Courtesy of Brian Kesterson.)

Under the conditions, the firefighters did a remarkable job preventing the spread of the fire, keeping it from consuming more of the city. Nathan's, a landmark clothing and shoe store at 225 Ann Street, was saved even though the adjacent buildings burned to the ground. (Courtesy of Brian Kesterson.)

This photograph of the confluence of the Little Kanawha and Ohio Rivers, dated March 30, 1913, shows a remarkable scene. That the riverboat *Ohio* struck the Ohio River Railroad Bridge with its bow was interesting enough. Upon closer examination, however, one sees that the *Ohio* hit the bridge from what had previously been dry land. The photograph also emphasizes the hazards of riverboat travel during the flood, which—along with the loss of overland routes—contributed to the isolation of much of the city. The spans of the B&O Bridge over the Ohio River are in the background. (Courtesy of Brian Kesterson.)

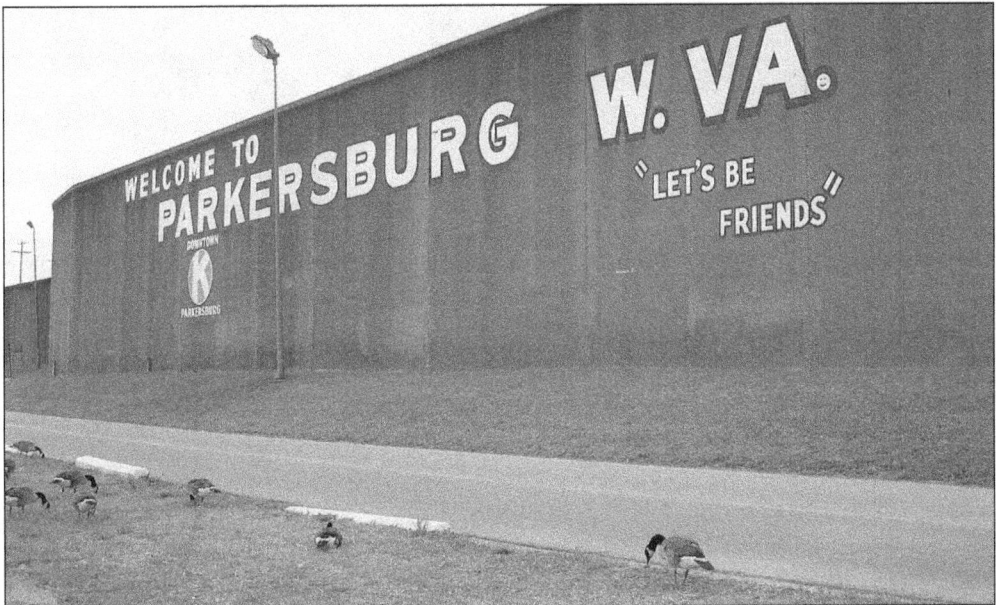

After more than 100 years of periodic flooding, the city moved forward with a plan to build a floodwall in 1946. The major project took four years and was completed in 1950. The floodwall extends from the Fifth Street Bridge along the Little Kanawha River to the Ohio River, where it continues to Thirty-fourth Street and Murdock Avenue, for a total of more than 3.75 miles of concrete and earthen levees. The wall required 63,000 cubic yards of concrete, more than 4,000 tons of steel, and more than 600,000 cubic yards of soil. The wall, with a height three feet higher than the 1913 crest, cost more than $6 million—approximately $53 million today—although Parkersburg was responsible for just $330,000—or nearly $3 million today. (Courtesy of Tim Kiser.)

Fire destroyed or made unsalvageable many local landmarks, including the beautiful old city hall in 1980, the Grand Hotel—in a 1945 fire with seven fatalities—and the B&O Roundhouse in 1989. The irreplaceable Camden Theater suffered the same fate on November 30, 1929. The fire that erupted around 7:30 p.m. quickly spread, and within three hours had engulfed an entire city block. Despite help from nearby Marietta, the fire burned through the night into the next afternoon and the theater was completely lost. Other businesses impacted by the fire, either damaged or lost, were the A&P Tea Store, Woolworth's, and the Dutch Oven. Despite the loss, positive steps came out of the tragedy—the city determined that the fire department needed money for new stations, modern equipment, and more firefighters—resulting in the nationally known, first-rate fire department of today. (Courtesy of Artcraft Studio.)

On September 21, 1959, Scott Lumber suffered a devastating fire at the company's warehouse at the foot of Sixth Street, with losses estimated to be near $100,000. The warehouse, described by the *Parkersburg News* as a "rather old two-story brick building," had previously been used by Parkersburg Ice Company for storage. A night watchman discovered the fire, not believed to be of suspicious origins, at 6:00 p.m., and notified the fire department. He and two managers in the building escaped unharmed. The intense blaze required all on-duty firefighters, and off-duty firefighters were called to help. Some off-duty firefighters complained that heavy traffic and an unusually large number of onlookers blocked their access to the fire. Although the warehouse and contents were considered an almost complete loss, firefighters prevented the fire from spreading to nearby buildings. (Both, courtesy of the PFD.)

Another historic fire destroyed a building with businesses and apartments on Seventh Street on January 8, 1984. Luckily, residents escaped the fire. Two residents attempted to put the fire out by themselves but realized more help was needed, calling the fire department around 3:00 p.m. A total of 17 firefighters responded, staying until 10:04 p.m. to ensure the fire was completely extinguished. The fire heavily damaged the building, causing about $175,000 in damage. Spectators saw an awe-inspiring sight, with flames burning through the windows of the upper two floors and the roof. Fire inspector Harold Barnhouse determined the fire was arson and a subsequent investigation led to an arrest and a confession. (Courtesy of the PFD.)

One of Parkersburg's most unusual catastrophes was the Quincy Hill water tank disaster. At about 5:10 a.m. on March 19, 1909, the city's two steel water tanks on Quincy Hill, which had been filled the night before to meet the morning demand, burst, sending approximately two million gallons of water rushing down the hill toward Avery Street. The manmade flash flood washed away houses and destroyed all but the front wall of St. John's Lutheran Church. The disaster also killed Walter and Flora Wigal instantly as they lay asleep in bed, and Katie Carnes, who died days later from her injuries. Many believed that worse damage was prevented by the well-built Lutheran church, which served as a break. The tanks, estimated to be 26 years old, probably burst because of corroded bolts holding together often-repaired steel plates. (Courtesy of Artcraft Studio.)

One of the worst snowstorms endured by the city was the Valentine's Day blizzard of 1940. Nearly 11 inches of snow fell—the second highest total in the city's history for February and the most that had fallen in four years. Half of the county's school students were unable to attend school on Wednesday, February 14, because of six-foot snowdrifts on secondary roads. The school board then cancelled school on Thursday and Friday, cancellations which, according to the *Parkersburg News*, were the "first to occur here within the memory of the superintendent." The heavy snow also caused public transportation to fall "behind schedule." The inconvenience proved to be short-lived as warmer temperatures in the high 30s and sunshine performed the bulk of the snow removal, "turning the deep snow to rapidly-melting slush." (Both, courtesy of the Library of Congress.)

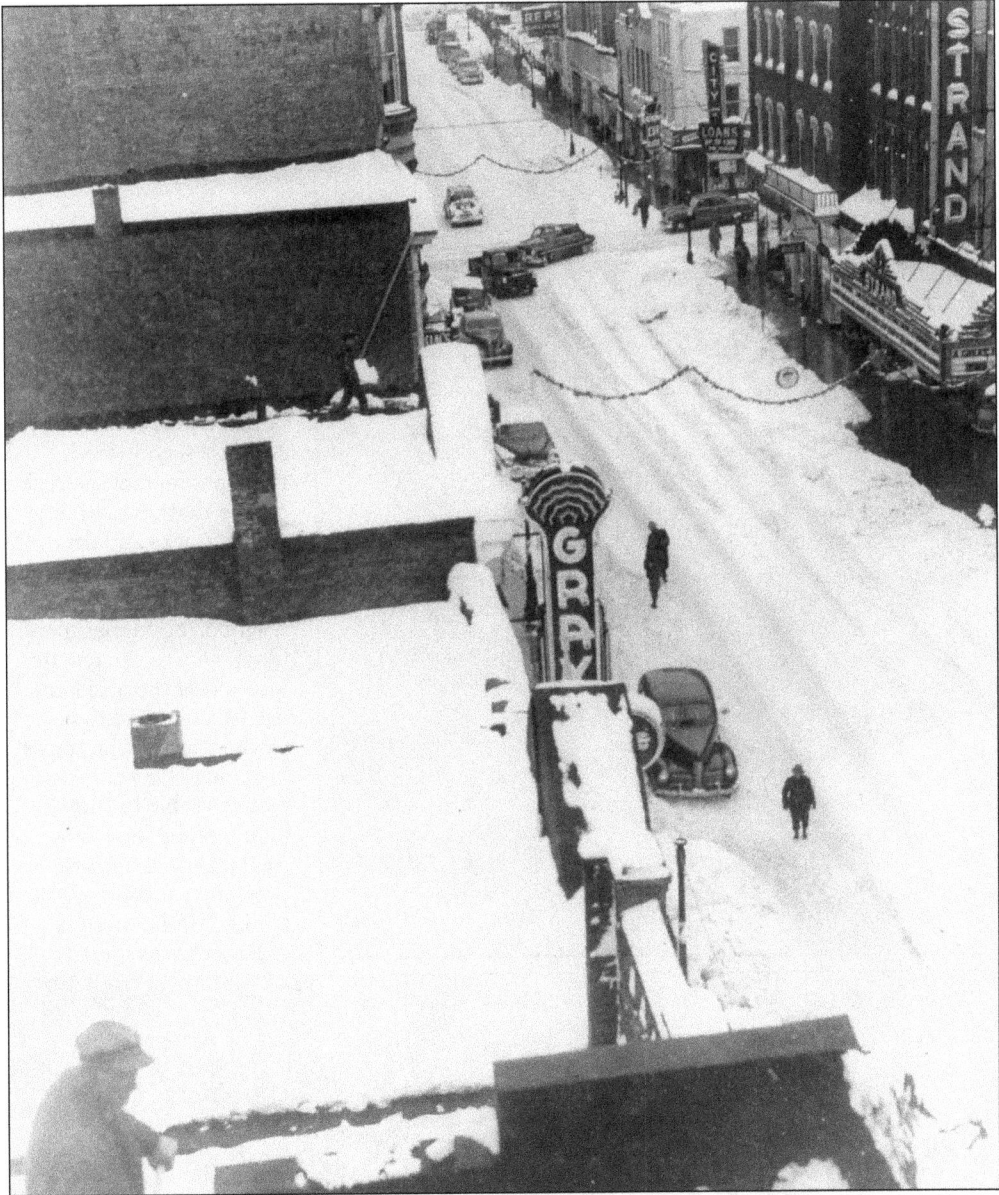

The single worst snow event in Parkersburg's history was the Great Appalachian Storm of 1950, which swept through on Thanksgiving weekend and dumped an amazing 34.4 inches of snow, with high temperatures only reaching the low teens and winds as high as 39 miles per hour. The heavy snowfall started on Saturday, November 25, and continued through Monday, closing stores and emptying the streets. Conditions halted local and long distance transportation, and even the B&O was running two and a half hours behind schedule. As late as Tuesday, the airport was still hoping to open a single runway. Schools were closed all week. Although the city planned a round-the-clock schedule to clear the streets, the start of the Christmas season made the commercial district so desperate that the Parkersburg Board of Commerce paid the city for extra trucks. The crushing storm proved to be a brief blast of winter, as by December 3, the high temperature reached an unseasonably warm 62 degrees and cleared the city of snow. (Courtesy of Artcraft Studio.)

Given that Parkersburg was both a river town and rail town, train wrecks were an unfortunate part of life. In 1920, Streetcar No. 623, seen in both these photographs, struck a mule that was standing on the tracks and derailed. The streetcar was traveling to Parkersburg from neighboring Marietta, Ohio. Due to the remote location of the accident, the streetcar had to be placed back on the tracks by hand. The wooden planks visible in the photographs show how the locals managed to hoist the car back on the tracks. (Both, courtesy of Brian Kesterson.)

Eight

SPORTS AND THE ARTS

Local baseball was extremely popular in Parkersburg, prompting the city to add lights in the early 1900s. Probably spurred on by the first night game in Major League Baseball in Cincinnati, lights were put up at Y Field at South Park. (Courtesy of Artcraft Studio.)

The city has hosted a number of exhibition baseball games. In 1896, the locals defeated the sixth-place Pittsburgh Pirates 6-4 when the Pirates, seen here in their 1896 team photograph, were managed by the legendary Connie Mack (third from left, second row). After the loss, Mack signed Parkersburg's Jack Taylor, who, according to the *Daily State Journal*, had "pitched a truly remarkable game," to play for his 1897 Milwaukee club. (Courtesy of Robert Anderson.)

Retired Pittsburgh Pirates great Honus Wagner (right) captained a touring baseball team from Pittsburgh—Green Cab—into Parkersburg probably in 1926. The player on the left is local standout Dick "Doc" Hoblitzell, who played for the Cincinnati Reds and Boston Red Sox before World War I, winning the World Series with the Red Sox in 1915 and 1916. (Courtesy of Bob Enoch.)

Parkersburg has fielded only a handful of minor league teams playing in recognized minor leagues. The shortest stint was by a team lasting just 11 games in the 1909 minor league Class D Pennsylvania–West Virginia league. Parkersburg had a team in 1910 as part of the new Class D Virginia Valley League, but that team lasted just one season. After 21 years without professional ball, Parkersburg was one of three cities to host a team—the Parkers—in 1931. More than six decades later, the Ohio Valley Redcoats were based at Parkersburg's Bennett Stump Field and played in the Frontier League as a charter member from 1993 to 1998 before moving on to other sites and finally disbanding in 2005. Seen here is a local town team, the Nationals, in the early 1900s. (Courtesy of Bob Enoch.)

Although the town was without a consistent professional presence, local merchants were proud to sponsor local teams. They figured prominently in the city's early-1900s baseball history. Businesses often used the common practice of employing men who were not too coincidentally also standout ballplayers, known as ringers. Players often traveled from town to town plying their trade. One of the businesses that regularly fielded a dominant team was American Viscose. Another very natural sponsor was Parkersburg Sporting Goods. Many games were played at South Side Park and Oak Park (now City Park). (Both, courtesy of Bob Enoch.)

Alfred Earl "Greasy" Neale was a multisport star at Parkersburg High School. He played eight years in the major leagues, helping the Cincinnati Reds win the 1919 "Black Sox" World Series. Neale also coached football successfully, leading Washington and Jefferson College to the 1921 Rose Bowl, where they played California to a 0-0 tie. He later coached the NFL's Philadelphia Eagles and was inducted into the Pro Football Hall of Fame in 1969. (Courtesy of the Library of Congress.)

Another Parkersburg coaching great was Ben Schwartzwalder. In his first five years after arriving in Parkersburg in 1936, Schwartzwalder had a record of 45-6-2, including an 11-0 record and a state football championship in 1938. Schwartzwalder landed at Syracuse University, where he coached football from 1949 to 1973, including an 11-0 national championship season in 1959. Schwartzwalder was inducted into the College Football Hall of Fame in 1982. (Courtesy of Artcraft Studio.)

The city's legacy of winning football was carried forward from Neale and Schwartzwalder by Buddy James. Coach James, a native of Parkersburg and a 1956 graduate of Parkersburg High School, became the head coach of his alma mater in 1968, a position he held until 1990. During his tenure, Coach James led the team to two state championships and a PHS-record 178 victories. The bedrocks of James's coaching philosophy were an emphasis on the teaching component and instilling self-discipline in players. These photographs show Coach James through the years, left in 1973, and below in an undated photograph later in his career. He has been enshrined in numerous halls of fame, including the Mid-Ohio Valley Sports Hall, which inducted him in 2002. (Both, courtesy of Buddy James.)

Buddy James had a spectacular playing career at PHS, winning selection as an all-state player his senior year. In this photograph, James (75) is pulling to throw a block. He first attended Montana State, winning a national championship as a freshman. With the Big Sky winter as encouragement, James returned home to finish his career at Marshall University. As PHS coach, James coached teams to four football state championship games, winning two in 1976 and 1978. James's championship teams were rock solid on defense; in each championship year, PHS defeated DuPont by a combined score of 36-0. PHS's football legacy is being carried on by the quarterback of Coach James's 1978 team, Don Reeves, who, in addition to coaching, has been a driving force behind the PHS Football Hall of Fame. (Courtesy of Buddy James and the PHS Football Hall of Fame.)

Segregated Sumner High fielded this team in 1902. Like most teams from this era of football, they had few players and no helmets or pads. The only protective gear available to the players were the nose guards hanging around the necks of several players. Sumner football player and graduate Arnett "Ace" Mumford, a 2001 College Football Hall of Fame inductee, had a stellar coaching career. After graduation, he attended Wilberforce College before moving on to Southern University and leading them to five Black College National Championships between 1936 and 1961. During that stretch, the team had a 38-game winning streak. (Courtesy of Artcraft Studio.)

By the early 20th century, basketball was becoming popular for participants and spectators. In 1914, West Virginia began holding tournaments and recognizing state high school championships, the first sport to do so. Parkersburg High School won its first state championship in 1916 and again in 1917. The school's success and popularity caused local leagues to form at such venues as the YMCA. With local sporting events typically being the only ones most people could attend, leagues proliferated all over the country at that time. Local teams included the Mountain State Business College (above in 1914) and the Parkersburg First Christian Church (below in 1922). Much like football, the local basketball teams played with a minimum of equipment and players. (Both, courtesy of Artcraft Studio.)

Parkersburg has also hosted numerous exhibitions of a variety of sports. In the late 1960s, American gymnastics great and Olympian Muriel Grossfeld gave an exhibition at a local high school. A driving force to expand interest in American gymnastics, Grossfeld gave performances like this to bring attention to the sport. Her resume was certainly unimpeachable: she was the first American woman to be a three-time Olympian and was a 19-time American national champion. After retiring from competition, Grossfeld went on to become a coach and a judge; she is believed to be the first person from any sport or country to participate in the Olympic Games as an athlete, a coach, and a judge. She was inducted into the United States Gymnastics Hall of Fame in 1981. (Courtesy of the Spencer family of Glendale Gym.)

Parkersburg has produced its own group of accomplished gymnasts, including Jerry Spencer, who was a standout gymnast at Parkersburg High School before attending West Virginia University on an athletic scholarship. At WVU, Spencer won acclaim, finishing seventh nationally in the parallel bars. Afterward, he and his wife, Danny, started Glendale Gym in Wood County. Spencer was selected for the Mid-Ohio Valley Sports Hall of Fame in 2010. In these photographs, Spencer performs on the parallel bars and poses (kneeling, on left) with his WVU teammates. (Both, photographs by Richard Phillips, courtesy of the Richard Phillips family, from the collection of the Spencer family of Glendale Gym.)

Janet Funderburk, a 1982 graduate of Parkersburg High School and a member of Spencer's Glendale Gym, was—at age 14—the youngest American ever to qualify for the Olympic Trials. Funderburk chose to pass on the opportunity, but her decision was a moot point anyway because the United States boycotted the 1980 Moscow Olympics in protest of the Soviet Union's invasion of Afghanistan. While a student at PHS, Funderburk returned to competitive gymnastics at Glendale Gym and earned an athletic scholarship to West Virginia University. She set records at WVU that lasted for more than a decade. These photographs show Funderburk in practice at Glendale (left) with Linda Bussey, the first USA Gymnastic West Virginia State Chair, and competing at WVU (below). (Both, courtesy of the Spencer family of Glendale Gym.)

Parkersburg has a long and illustrious history of high school athletics. The city was recognized by ESPN in 2008 in the national TitleTown contest. Despite not having a consistent professional presence, Parkersburg still earned second place as voted on by fans. The city's high schools have won 192 West Virginia state championships in various sports: 137 by PHS, 38 by PSHS, and 17 by Parkersburg Catholic. The PHS boys' basketball team won the first state championship in 1916, and the first girls' championship won by a city school was the 1970 PHS tennis team. This marker was placed near the Parkersburg traffic circle to commemorate ESPN's recognition of the city's athletic achievements. (Courtesy of Robert Anderson.)

The 1980 Parkersburg South High School Cross Country state championship team, seen here, was the beginning of a dynasty. Although the team did not win the championship in 1981, they won consecutive titles in 1982, 1983, and 1984, giving them four championships in five years. (Courtesy of Rick Leach and PSHS.)

Sports were often used for local fundraising. In the late 1970s and early 1980s, Parkersburg Community College's staff council organized a run known as OctoberFAST. Participants ran 4.2 miles to a campus finish line, where beer was provided by a local distributor. The competition was serious—one professor even collapsed on the course and was taken to the hospital. This photograph is from the inaugural event. (Courtesy of Dennis Bell and WVU at Parkersburg.)

124

Residents of Parkersburg often had to find low-cost ways to entertain themselves. Bowling was a popular sport in the area due to its social nature and low cost. Parkersburg hosted many bowling alleys, including this one inside the Coliseum, Emerson Bowling Alley on the north side of Parkersburg, and Ren-Dor Bowling Lanes on the south side of Parkersburg. While the Coliseum was closed and its lanes were removed, both Emerson and Ren-Dor are still operating today. (Courtesy of Artcraft Studio.)

Lily Irene Jackson, the daughter of judge John J. Jackson Jr., was a popular socialite from Parkersburg who became famous for her artistic ability. She was known for portraits, particularly of animals and floral arrangements. Jackson promoted the arts in Parkersburg and was a founding member of the Parkersburg Art Society. Upon her death in 1928, she donated her art to the city of Parkersburg on the condition that the city build an art gallery for it. Unfortunately, the city elected not to build the gallery and her work was sold at auction. Recently, local historians, with help from the Blennerhassett Museum, have been collecting the work and putting it on display. (Courtesy of Brian Kesterson.)

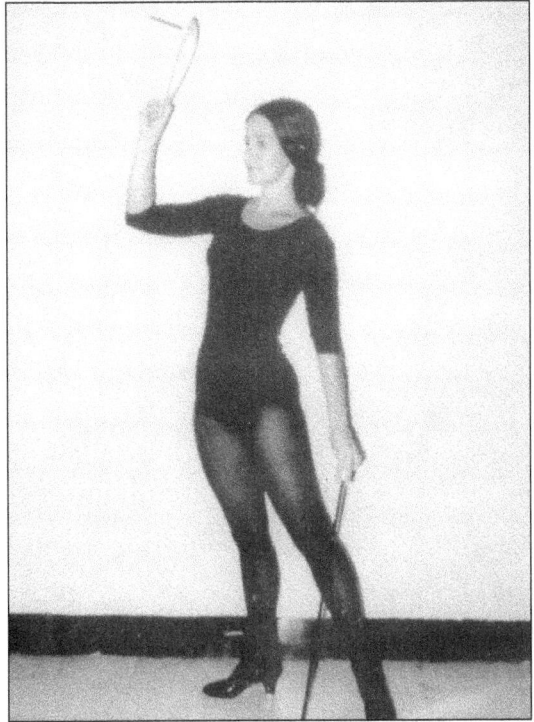

Norma Gunter touched the lives of many aspiring dancers in Parkersburg. Originally from Beckley, Gunter settled in Parkersburg and taught dance to children and adults at her studio in the former Nash School building for more than 50 years. She trained and provided dancers for the inaugural performance of Theatre West Virginia's *Honey in the Rock* in 1961. Among the dancers in that first show was Gunter's sister, Rosemary—below, on right, with Norma—herself an accomplished dancer and an accepted member of the famed Rockettes of New York City. Norma Gunter also established West Virginia's first professional touring dance company, the Mid-Ohio Valley Ballet Company. Her daughter, Suzy, now operates the studio and company, continuing her mother's legacy. (Both, courtesy of Suzy Gunter.)

Visit us at
arcadiapublishing.com

www.ingramcontent.com/pod-product-compliance
Lightning Source LLC
Chambersburg PA
CBHW050713110426
42813CB00007B/2171